AF200009

Impressum
Verlag: BABADADA GmbH, Nedderfeld 112 , 22529 Hamburg
Geschäftsführer / Verlagsleitung: Harald Hof
Druck: Books on Demand GmbH, In de Tarpen 42, 22848 Norderstedt

Imprint
Publisher: BABADADA GmbH, Nedderfeld 112 , 22529 Hamburg, Germany
Managing Director / Publishing direction: Harald Hof
Print: Books on Demand GmbH, In de Tarpen 42, 22848 Norderstedt

divide
bahagi

$186/2$

classroom
bilik darjah

board
papan

school yard
laman/taman sekolah

teacher
guru

paper
kertas

write
tulis

pen
pen

desk
meja

ruler
pembaris

book
buku

pupil
murid

satchel

beg galas

pencil case

kotak pensel

pencil

pensel

pencil sharpener

pengasah pensel

rubber

pemadam

drawing pad

kertas lukisan

drawing

melukis

paintbrush

berus lukis

paint box

kotak warna

scissors

gunting

glue

gam

exercise book

buku latihan

homework

kerja rumah

number

nombor

add

tambah

subtract

tolak

multiply

darab

calculate

kira

letter

huruf

alphabet

abjad

word

kata

text

teks

read

baca

chalk

kapur

lesson

pelajaran

register

daftar

examination

peperiksaan

certificate

sijil

school uniform

uniform sekolah

education

pendidikan

encyclopedia

ensiklopedia

university

universiti

microscope

mikroskop

map

peta

waste-paper basket

bakul sampah

hotel
hotel

hostel
asrama

currency exchange office
pejabat tukaran mata wang

car
kereta

language

bahasa

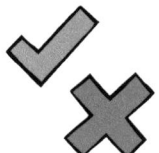

yes / no

ya / tidak

Okay

okey

hello

helo

translator

penterjemah

Thank you

Terima kasih

how much is...?

berapa banyak...?

I don´t get it

saya tidak faham

problem

masalah

Good evening!

Selamat petang!

Good morning!

Selamat Pagi!

Good night!

Selamat Malam!

goodbye

selamat tinggal

direction

arah

luggage

bagasi

bag

beg

backpack

beg galas

guest

tetamu

room

bilik tidur

sleeping bag

beg tidur

tent

khemah

tourist information

maklumat pelancong

beach

pantai

credit card

kad kredit

breakfast

sarapan

lunch

makan tengah hari

dinner

makan malam

Ticket

tiket

elevator

lif

stamp

setem

border

sempadan

customs

kastam

embassy

kedutaan

visa

visa

passport

pasport

airplane
kapal terbang

ship
kapal

fire truck
kereta bomba

truck
trak

bus
bas

motorboat
motobot

car
kereta

bike
basikal

ferry
feri

boat
bot

motorbike
motosikal

police car
kereta polis

racing car
kereta lumba

rental car
kereta sewa

car sharing

berkongsi kereta

tow truck

trak tunda

garbage truck

trak menolak

engine

motor

fuel

bahan api

fuel station

stesen minyak

traffic sign

tanda trafik

traffic

trafik

traffic jam

kesesakan lalu lintas

parking lot

tempat parkir

train station

stesen kereta api

tracks

trek

train

kereta api

tram

trem

wagon

gerabak

helicopter

helikopter

airport

lapangan terbang

tower

Menara

passenger

penumpang

container

bekas

carton

kadbod

cart

kart

basket

bakul

take off / land

berlepas / mendarat

city

bandar

village

kampung

city center

pusat bandar

house

rumah

movie theater / pawagam

advert / iklan

street light / lampu jalan

CINEMA

street / jalan

taxi / teksi

snack shop / kedai makanan ringan

pedestrian / pejalan kaki

sidewalk / turapan

zebra crossing / lintasan zebra

dumpster / tong sampah

crossing / lintasan

traffic lights / lampu isyarat

hut

pondok

apartment

flat

train station

stesen kereta api

city hall

dewan bandar

museum

muzium

school

sekolah

university

universiti

bank

bank

hospital

hospital

hotel

hotel

pharmacy

farmasi

office

pejabat

book shop

kedai buku

shop

kedai

flower shop

kedai bunga

supermarket

pasar raya

market

pasaran

department store

gedung

fishmonger's shop

penjual ikan

mall

pusat membeli-belah

harbor

pelabuhan

park

taman

bench

bangku

bridge

jambatan

stairs

tangga

subway

bawah tanah

tunnel

terowong

bus stop

hentian bas

bar

bar

restaurant

restoran

postbox

peti surat

street sign

papan tanda jalan

parking meter

meter parkir

zoo

zoo

swimming pool

kolam renang

mosque

masjid

farm

ladang

pollution

pencemaran

cemetery

tanah perkuburan

church

gereja

playground

taman permainan

temple

kuil

landscape

landskap

signpost
tiang tanda

path
jalan

meadow
padang rumput

stone
batu

hiker
pejalan kaki

tree
pokok

river
sungai

grass
rumput

flower
bunga

valley

lembah

hill

bukit

lake

tasik

forest

hutan

desert

padang pasir

volcano

gunung berapi

castle

istana

rainbow

pelangi

mushroom

cendawan

palm tree

pokok kelapa sawit

mosquito

nyamuk

fly

terbang

ant

semut

bee

lebah

spider

labah-labah

landscape - landskap

beetle

kumbang

frog

katak

squirrel

tupai

hedgehog

landak

hare

arnab

owl

burung hantu

bird

burung

swan

angsa

boar

babi jantan

deer

rusa

moose

moose

dam

empangan

wind turbine

turbin angin

solar panel

panel solar

climate

iklim

waiter
pelayan

menu
menu

chair
kerusi

soup
sup

pizza
piza

cutlery
kutleri

tablecloth
alas meja

starter
pemula

main course
hidangan utama

dessert
pencuci mulut

drinks
minuman

food
makanan

bottle
botol

fast food

makanan segera

street food

makanan jalanan

teapot

teko

sugar bowl

mangkuk gula

portion

bahagian

espresso machine

mesin espreso

high chair

kerusi tinggi

bill

bil

tray

dulang

knife

pisau

fork

garfu

spoon

sudu

teaspoon

sudu teh

serviette

serviette

glass

gelas

plate

pinggan

soup plate

mangkuk sup

saucer

piring

sauce

sos

salt shaker

tempat garam

pepper mill

pengisar lada

vinegar

cuka

oil

minyak

spices

rempah

ketchup

sos

mustard

mustard

mayonnaise

mayones

special offer
tawaran istimewa

customer
pelanggan

dairy products
tenusu

FOR

fruit
buah-buahan

shopping cart
troli

butcher's shop

tukang daging

bakery

kedai roti

weigh

berat

vegetables

sayur-sayuran

meat

daging

frozen food

makanan sejuk beku

cold cuts

daging sejuk

canned food

makanan dalam tin

detergent

serbuk pencuci

candy

gula-gula

household products

produk isi rumah

cleaning products

produk pembersihan

sales representative

orang jualan

cash register

daftar tunai

cashier

juruwang

shopping list

senarai membeli-belah

opening hours

waktu pembukaan

wallet

beg duit

credit card

kad kredit

bag

beg

plastic bag

beg plastik

water
....
air

juice
....
jus

milk
....
susu

coke
....
kola

wine
....
wain

beer
....
bir

alcohol
....
alkohol

cocoa
....
koko

tea
....
the

coffee
....
kopi

espresso
....
espreso

cappuccino
....
kapucino

banana

pisang

apple

epal

orange

oren

melon

tembikai

lemon

lemon

carrot

lobak merah

garlic

bawang putih

bamboo

buluh

onion

bawang

mushroom

cendawan

nuts

kacang

noodles

mi

spaghetti

spageti

rice

nasi

salad

salad

fries

kerepek

fried potatoes

kentang goreng

pizza

piza

hamburger

hamburger

sandwich

sandwic

escalope

kutlet

ham

ham

salami

salami

sausage

sosej

chicken

ayam

roast

panggang

fish

ikan

porridge oats

bubur oat

muesli

muesli

cornflakes

emping jagung

flour

tepung

croissant

kroisan

bread roll

roti roll

bread

roti

toast

roti bakar

cookies

biskut

butter

mentega

curd

dadih

cake

kek

egg

telur

fried egg

telur goreng

cheese

keju

ice cream

ais krim

sugar

gula

honey

madu

jelly

jem

nougat cream

krim nougat

curry

kari

goat

kambing

cow

lembu

calf

anak lembu

pig

babi

piglet

anak babi

bull

lembu

goose

angsa

duck

itik

chick

anak ayam

hen

ayam betina

cockerel

ayam jantan muda

rat

tikus

cat

kucing

mouse

tikus

ox

lembu jantan

dog

anjing

dog house

rumah anjing

garden hose

hos taman

watering can

bekas siraman

scythe

sabit

plow

bajak

sickle

sabit

hoe

cangkul

pitchfork

serampang peladang

axe

kapak

pushcart

kereta sorong

trough

palung

milk can

tin susu

sack

karung

fence

pagar

stable

stabil

greenhouse

rumah hijau

soil

tanah

seed

benih

fertilizer

baja

combine harvester

jentuai

harvest

tuai

harvest

menuai

yams

keladi

wheat

gandum

soya

soya

potato

kentang

corn

jagung

rapeseed

biji sawi

fruit tree

pokok buah-buahan

manioc

ubi kayu

grain

bijirin

living room

ruang tamu

bathroom

bilik air

kitchen

dapur

bedroom

bilik tidur

kids room

bilik kanak-kanak

dining room

ruang makan

floor

lantai

wall

dinding

ceiling

siling

cellar

bilik bawah tanah

sauna

sauna

balcony

balkoni

terrace

teres

pool

kolam renang

lawn mower

pemotong rumput

sheet

lembaran

bedspread

penutup tilam

bed

katil

broom

penyapu

bucket

timba

switch

suis

carpet

permaidani

drape

tirai

table

meja

chair

kerusi

rocking chair

kerusi malas

armchair

kerusi

book

buku

blanket

selimut

decoration

hiasan

firewood

kayu api

film

filem

stereo system

hi-fi

key

kunci

newspaper

akhbar

painting

lukisan

poster

poster

radio

radio

notebook

buku catatan

vacuum cleaner

penyedut habuk

cactus

kaktus

candle

lilin

fridge
peti sejuk

microwave oven
ketuhar gelombang mikro

kitchen scales
penimbang dapur

toaster
pembakar roti

laundry detergent
bahan pencuci

stove
oven

freezer
penyejuk beku

dishwasher
pembasuh pinggan mangkuk

cooker
periuk dapur

pot
periuk

cast-iron pot
periuk besi

wok / kadai
kuali

pan
pan

kettle
cerek

steamer

pengukus

baking tray

dulang pembakar

crockery

pinggan mangkuk

mug

koleh

bowl

mangkuk

chopsticks

penyepit

ladle

senduk

spatula

spatula

whisk

pengadun

strainer

penapis

sieve

ayak

grater

pemarut

mortar

mortar

barbecue

barbeku

fireplace

pembakaran terbuka

chopping board

papan pencincang

rolling pin

pin golekan

corkscrew

skru gabus

can

tin

can opener

pembuka tin

oven cloth

pemegang periuk

sink

sinki

brush

berus

sponge

span

blender

pengisar

deep freezer

penyejuk beku

baby bottle

botol bayi

tap

paip

kitchen - dapur

heating
pemanasan

shower
mandi

towel
tuala

shower curtain
tirai mandi

bubble bath
mandi buih

bathtub
tab mandi

glass
gelas

washing machine
mesin basuh

tiles
jubin

tap
paip

potty
tandas

sink
sinki

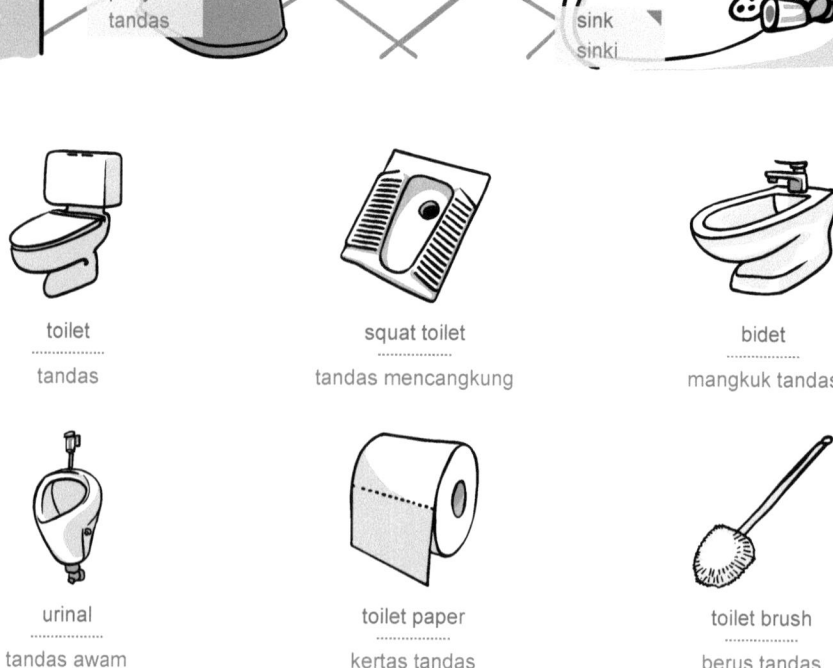

toilet
tandas

squat toilet
tandas mencangkung

bidet
mangkuk tandas

urinal
tandas awam

toilet paper
kertas tandas

toilet brush
berus tandas

toothbrush

berus gigi

toothpaste

ubat gigi

dental floss

flos gigi

wash

cuci

hand shower

mandian tangan

douche

pancuran

basin

besen

back brush

belakang berus

soap

sabun

shower gel

gel mandian

shampoo

syampu

flannel

flanel

drain

longkang

creme

krim

deodorant

deodoran

mirror

cermin

hand mirror

cermin tangan

razor

pisau cukur

shaving foam

busa cukur

aftershave

selepas cukur

comb

sikat

brush

berus

hair-dryer

pengering rambut

hairspray

semburan rambut

makeup

mekap

lipstick

gincu

nail varnish

varnis kuku

cotton wool

bulu kapas

nail scissors

gunting kuku

perfume

pewangi

washbag

beg basuhan

stool

bangku

weighing scales

skala berat

bathrobe

jubah mandi

rubber gloves

sarung tangan getah

tampon

kapas

sanitary towel

tuala wanita

chemical toilet

tandas kimia

alarm clock
jam loceng

cuddly toy
mainan kegemaran

toy car
kereta mainan

rattle
kerincing bayi

doll's house
rumah anak patung

present
hadiah

balloon

belon

bed

katil

stroller

kereta sorong bayi

deck of cards

set kad

jigsaw

susun suai gambar

comic

komik

lego bricks

batu bata lego

toy blocks

blok mainan

action figure

figura aksi

romper suit

baju bayi

frisbee

frisbee

mobile

mainan bayi mudah alih

board game

permainan papan

dice

dadu

model train set

set model kereta api

pacifier

palsu

party

parti

picture book

buku bergambar

ball

bola

doll

anak patung

play

main

sandpit

lubang pasir

swing

buai

toys

mainan

video game console

konsol permainan video

tricycle

basikal roda tiga

teddy bear

anak patung beruang

wardrobe

almari pakaian

clothing

pakaian

socks

stoking

stockings

stoking

tights

ketat

scarf
skarf

umbrella
payung

t-shirt
kemeja-t

keselamatan

boots
but

slippers
selipar

sneakers
kasut sukan

sandals
sandal

shoes
kasut

rubber boots
but getah

underwear
seluar dalam

bra
coli

undershirt
ves

body

badan

pants

Seluar panjang

jeans

jean

skirt

skirt

blouse

blaus

shirt

kemeja

pullover

baju panas sarung

sweater

sweater

blazer

blazer

jacket

jaket

coat

kot

raincoat

baju hujan

costume

kostum

dress

pakaian

wedding dress

baju pengantin

suit

sut

nightgown

baju tidur

pajamas

baju tidur

sari

sari

headscarf

skarf kepala

turban

serban

burka

burqa

kaftan

kaftan

abaya

abaya/jubah

swimsuit

baju renang

trunks

seluar renang

shorts

seluar pendek

tracksuit

sut balapan

apron

apron

gloves

sarung tangan

button

butang

glasses

cermin mata

bracelet

gelang tangan

necklace

rantai leher

ring

cincin

earring

subang

cap

topi

coat hanger

penyangkut kot

hat

topi

tie

tali leher

zip

zip

helmet

topi keledar

braces

pendakap

school uniform

uniform sekolah

uniform

seragam

bib

lapik dada

pacifier

palsu

diaper

lampin

server
pelayan

filing cabinet
kabinet fail

printer
mesin pencetak

monitor
monitor

paper
kertas

desk
meja

mouse
tetikus

folder
folder

keyboard
papan kekunci

chair
kerusi

waste-paper basket
bakul sampah

computer
komputer

coffee mug

cawan kopi

calculator

kalkulator

internet

internet

laptop

komputer riba

letter

surat

message

mesej

cell phone

mudah alih

network

rangkaian

photocopier

mesin fotokopi

software

perisian

telephone

telefon

plug socket

soket plag

fax machine

mesin faks

form

bentuk

document

dokumen

buy

beli

pay

bayar

trade

berdagang

money

wang

dollar

dolar

euro

euro

yen

yen

rouble

rubel

Swiss franc

franc swiss

renminbi yuan

renminbi yuan

rupee

rupee

cash point

mata tunai

currency exchange office

pejabat tukaran mata wang

gold

emas

silver

perak

oil

minyak

energy

tenaga

price

harga

contract

kontrak

tax

cukai

stock

stok

work

kerja

employee

pekerja

employer

majikan

factory

kilang

shop

kedai

police officer
pegawai polis

fireman
ahli bomba

pilot
juruterbang

cook
tukang masak

doctor
doktor

gardener

tukang kebun

carpenter

tukang kayu

seamstress

tukang jahit

judge

hakim

chemist

ahli kimia

actor

pelakon

bus driver

pemandu bas

taxi driver

pemandu teksi

fisherman

nelayan

cleaning lady

wanita pencuci

roofer

kasau

waiter

pelayan

hunter

pemburu

painter

pelukis

baker

bakeri

electrician

juruelektrik

builder

pembangun

engineer

jurutera

butcher

penjual daging

plumber

tukang paip

postman

posmen

soldier

askar

architect

arkitek

cashier

juruwang

florist

kedai bunga

hairdresser

pendandan rambut

conductor

konduktor

mechanic

mekanik

captain

kapten

dentist

doktor gigi

scientist

ahli sains

rabbi

tuhanku

imam

imam

monk

sami

pastor

paderi

hammer
tukul

pliers
playar

screwdriver
pemutar skru

wrench
sepana

torch
obor

excavator

pengorek

toolbox

kotak peralatan

ladder

tangga

saw

gergaji

nails

kuku

drill

gerudi

repair
baiki

shovel
penyodok

Damn!
Celaka!

dustpan
penadah sampah

paint can
periuk cat

screws
skru

musical instruments
alat muzik

drum set
perangkat dram

loud speaker
pembesar suara

guitar
gitar

double bass
bass berganda

trumpet
trompet

piano

piano

violin

biola

bass

bass

timpani

timpani

drums

dram

keyboard

papan kekunci

saxophone

saksofon

flute

seruling

microphone

mikrofon

entrance
pintu masuk

tiger
harimau

cage
sangkar

zebra
zebra

animal feed
makanan haiwan

panda
panda

animals
haiwan

elephant
gajah

kangaroo
kanggaru

rhino
badak sumbu

gorilla
gorila

bear
beruang

camel

unta

ostrich

burung unta

lion

singa

monkey

monyet

flamingo

flamingo

parrot

nuri

polar bear

beruang kutub

penguin

penguin

shark

yu

peacock

merak

snake

ular

crocodile

buaya

zookeeper

penjaga zoo

seal

anjing laut

jaguar

jaguar

pony

kuda

leopard

harimau

hippo

badak air

giraffe

zirafah

eagle

helang

boar

babi jantan

fish

ikan

turtle

penyu

walrus

anjing laut

fox

musang

gazelle

rusa

American football
bola sepak Amerika

cycling
berbasikal

tennis
tenis

basketball
bola keranjang

swimming
renang

boxing
tinju

ice hockey
hoki ais

soccer
bola sepak

badminton
badminton

athletics
olahraga

handball
bola baling

skiing
ski

polo
polo

jump
lompat

laugh
ketawa

hug
peluk

walk
berjalan

sing
menyanyi

dream
mimpi

pray
berdoa

kiss
cium

write
tulis

draw
lukis

show
tunjuk

push
tolak

give
beri

take
ambil

have
ada

do
buat

be
ialah

stand
berdiri

run
lari

pull
tarik

throw
buang

fall
jatuh

lie
tipu

wait
tunggu

carry
bawa

sit
duduk

get dressed
pakai

sleep
tidur

wake up
bangkit

look at

lihat pada

cry

menangis

stroke

strok

comb

sikat

talk

cakap

understand

faham

ask

tanya

listen

dengar

drink

minum

eat

makan

tidy up

mengemas

love

sayang

cook

masak

drive

pandu

fly

terbang

sail
belayar

calculate
kira

read
baca

learn
belajar

work
kerja

marry
nikah

sew
jahit

brush teeth
memberus gigi

kill
bunuh

smoke
asap

send
hantar

grandmother
nenek

grandfather
datuk

father
bapa

mother
ibu

baby
bayi

daughter
anak perempuan

son
anak lelaki

guest

tetamu

aunt

mak cik

uncle

pak cik

brother

abang

sister

kakak

forehead
dahi

eye
mata

shoulder
bahu

finger
jari

face
muka

chin
dagu

hand
tangan

breast
dada

leg
kaki

arm
lengan

baby

bayi

man

lelaki

woman

wanita

girl

perempuan

boy

lelaki

head

kepala

back

belakang

belly

bawah perut

navel

pusat

toe

jari kaki

heel

tumit

bone

tulang

hip

pinggul

knee

lutut

elbow

siku

nose

hidung

buttocks

bawah

skin

kulit

cheek

pipi

ear

telinga

lip

bibir

mouth

mulut

tooth

gigi

tongue

lidah

brain

otak

heart

hati

muscle

otot

lung

paru-paru

liver

hati

stomach

perut

kidneys

buah pinggang

sex

seks

condom

kondom

ovum

faraj

semen

mani

pregnancy

mengandung

menstruation

haid

vagina

faraj

penis

penis

eyebrow

kening

hair

rambut

neck

leher

body - badan

hospital
hospital

ambulance
ambulans

wheelchair
kerusi roda

fracture
patah tulang

doctor
doktor

emergency room
bilik kecemasan

nurse
jururawat

emergency
kecemasan

unconscious
tak sedar

pain
sakit

injury

kecederaan

bleeding

pendarahan

heart attack

serangan jantung

stroke

strok

allergy

alergi

cough

batuk

fever

demam

flu

selesema

diarrhea

cirit-birit

headache

sakit kepala

cancer

kanser

diabetes

diabetes

surgeon

pakar bedah

scalpel

pisau bedah

operation

pembedahan

CT

CT

x-ray

x-ray

ultrasound

ultrabunyi

face mask

topeng muka

disease

penyakit

waiting room

bilik menunggu

crutch

penongkat

plaster

plaster

bandage

pembalut

injection

suntikan

stethoscope

stetoskop

stretcher

pengusung

clinical thermometer

termometer klinik

birth

kelahiran

overweight

berat badan berlebihan

hearing aid

alat pendengaran

disinfectant

disinfektan

infection

jangkitan

virus

virus

HIV / AIDS

HIV / AIDS

medicine

perubatan

vaccination

vaksinasi

tablets

tablet

pill

pil

emergency call

panggilan kecemasan

blood pressure monitor

pantau tekanan darah

ill / healthy

sakit / sihat

Help!

Tolong!

alarm

penggera

assault

serang

attack

serangan

danger

bahaya

emergency exit

pintu kecemasan

Fire!

Api!

fire extinguisher

alat pemadam api

accident

kemalangan

first-aid kit

alat pertolongan cemas

SOS

SOS

police

polis

Europe

Eropah

North America

Amerika Utara

South America

Amerika Selatan

Africa

Afrika

Asia

Asia

Australia

Australia

Atlantic

Atlantic

Pacific

Pasifik

Indian Ocean

Lautan Hindi

Antarctic Ocean

Lautan Antartik

Arctic Ocean

Lautan Artik

North pole

Kutub utara

South pole
Kutub Selatan

Antarctica
Antartika

earth
bumi

land
tanah

sea
laut

island
pulau

nation
negara

state
negeri

clock face

muka jam

hour hand

tangan jam

minute hand

tangan minit

second hand

terpakai

What time is it?

Jam berapa sekarang

day

hari

time

masa

now

sekarang

digital watch

jam digital

minute

minit

hour

jam

week

minggu

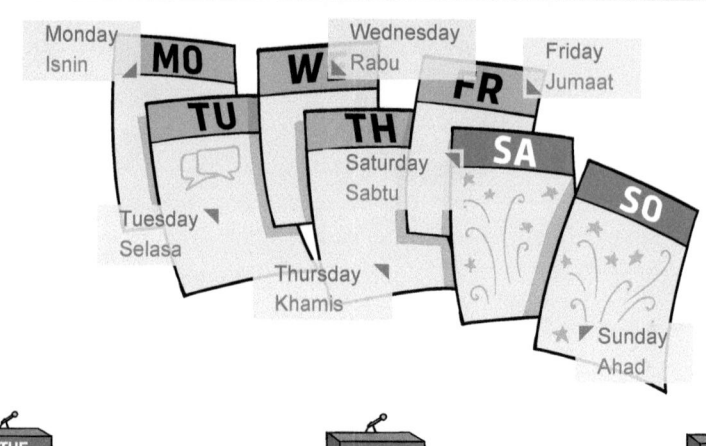

Monday
Isnin

Wednesday
Rabu

Friday
Jumaat

Tuesday
Selasa

Saturday
Sabtu

Thursday
Khamis

Sunday
Ahad

yesterday

semalam

today

hari ini

tomorrow

esok

morning

pagi

noon

tengah hari

evening

petang

workdays

hari kerja

weekend

hari minggu

rain
hujan

snow
salji

wind
angin

spring
musim bunga

fall
musim luruh

summer
musim panas

winter
musim salji

weather forecast

ramalan cuaca

thermometer

termometer

sunshine

sinar matahari

cloud

awan

fog

kabus

humidity

lembapan

lightning

kilat

thunder

petir

storm

ribut

hail

hujan batu

monsoon

monsun

flood

banjir

ice

ais

January

Januari

February

Februari

March

Mac

April

April

May

Mei

June

Jun

July

Julai

August

Ogos

year - tahun

September
September

October
Oktober

November
November

December
Disember

shapes
bentuk

circle
bulatan

square
petak

rectangle
segi empat tepat

triangle
segitiga

sphere
sfera

cube
kiub

white

putih

yellow

kuning

orange

oren

pink

merah jambu

red

merah

purple

ungu

blue

biru

green

hijau

brown

coklat

gray

kelabu

black

hitam

a lot / a little

banyak / sedikit

angry / calm

marah / tenang

beautiful / ugly

cantik / hodoh

beginning / end

bermula / tamat

big / small

besar kecil

bright / dark

terang / gelap

brother / sister

abang / kakak

clean / dirty

bersih / kotor

complete / incomplete

lengkap / tidak lengkap

day / night

hari / malam

dead / alive

mati / hidup

wide / narrow

luas / sempit

edible / inedible

boleh dimakan / tidak boleh dimakan

evil / kind

jahat / baik

excited / bored

teruja / bosan

fat / thin

gemuk / kurus

first / last

pertama / terakhir

friend / enemy

kawan / musuh

full / empty

penuh / kosong

hard / soft

keras / lembut

heavy / light

berat / ringan

hunger / thirst

lapar / dahaga

ill / healthy

sakit / sihat

illegal / legal

menyalahi undang-undang / undang-undang

intelligent / stupid

pintar / bodoh

left / right

kiri / kanan

near / far

dekat / jauh

new / used

baru / lama

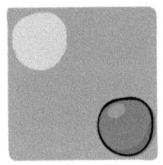

nothing / something

tiada / sesuatu

old / young

tua / muda

on / off

hidup / mati

open / closed

terbuka / tertutup

quiet / loud

diam / bising

rich / poor

kaya / miskin

right / wrong

betul / salah

rough / smooth

kasar / halus

sad / happy

sedih / gembira

short / long

pendek / panjang

slow / fast

lambat / laju

wet / dry

basah / kering

warm / cool

panas / sejuk

war / peace

berperang / berdamai

opposites - berlawanan

numbers
nombor

0	**1**	**2**
zero	one	two
sifar	satu	dua
3	**4**	**5**
three	four	five
tiga	empat	lima
6	**7**	**8**
six	seven	eight
enam	tujuh	lapan
9	**10**	**11**
nine	ten	eleven
sembilan	sepuluh	sebelas

12

twelve

dua belas

13

thirteen

tiga belas

14

fourteen

empat belas

15

fifteen

lima belas

16

sixteen

enam belas

17

seventeen

tujuh belas

18

eighteen

lapan belas

19

nineteen

Sembilan belas

20

twenty

dua puluh

100

hundred

ratus

1.000

thousand

ribu

1.000.000

million

juta

languages
bahasa-bahasa

English

Bahasa Inggeris

American English

Bahasa Inggeris Amerika

Chinese Mandarin

Bahasa Cina Mandarin

Hindi

Bahasa Hindi

Spanish

Bahasa Sepanyol

French

Bahasa Perancis

Arabic

Bahasa Arab

Russian

Bahasa Rusia

Portuguese

Bahasa Portugis

Bengali

Bahasa Benggali

German

Bahasa Jerman

Japanese

Bahasa Jepun

I

saya

you

anda

he / she / it

dia / dia / ia

we

kita

you

anda

they

mereka

who?

siapa?

what?

apa?

how?

bagaimana?

where?

di mana?

when?

bila?

name

nama

behind

belakang

in

dalam

in front of

di hadapan

over

lebih

on

pada

under

di bawah

beside

bersebelahan

between

antara

place

tempat